QUOTABLE
JOHN PAUL II

QUOTABLE
JOHN PAUL II

*Words of Wisdom, Faith, Solidarity, and Salvation
by and about* JOHN PAUL II, *a Pope for the 20th Century
and the New Millennium*

MIKE TOWLE

TowleHouse Publishing
Nashville, Tennessee

Library of Congress Cataloging-in-Publication data is available.
ISBN: 1-931249-24-5

TowleHouse books are distributed by National Book Network (NBN),
4720 Boston Way, Lanham, Maryland 20706.

Cover design by Gore Studio, Inc.
Page design by Mike Towle

Printed in the United States of America
1 2 3 4 5 6 — 07 06 05 04 03

CONTENTS

To all the fine folks who over the years have worshipped and shared fellowship at All Saints Church in Richford, Vermont

PREFACE

Until John Paul II came along, the papacy was the Catholic Church's great mystery—an elected position served by a man without a last name, known to the world only by a first name that really wasn't his. We could never really know him, or what he was like as a person. Where did he come from? How did he get there? Does he converse with God? Is he the final biblical authority, and, if so, why? How do you become pope, and do you suppose he cheers, cheers for ol' Notre Dame? What does he like to eat? Who listens to his confession?

Catechism in the sixties and seventies taught us that the pope was, for all practical purposes, God as man, giving homilies to rapt crowds routinely numbering in the hundreds of thousands. If the pope wasn't appointed by God, he at least embraced his vocation as a go-between for about a billion earthbound Catholics and almighty God. He was the president, Billy Graham, and the apostle Paul rolled up into one, and he called the Vatican home. His homilies could be touching, but he was untouchable.

That changed in 1978, when Karol Wojtyla was urgently elected pope as a darkhorse candidate to succeed the charismatic John Paul I, who had died in his sleep just a month into his papacy. Wojtyla's sudden ascension to the papacy was hailed as remarkable. Here he was, the world's first Polish pope, not a punch line to a joke, but real flesh and blood, as capable of schussing down the slopes of Kitzbuhel as he was rendering proper penance to a wide spectrum of sinners.

A hale, hearty, and robust fifty-eight when he became pope, John Paul II had the ruddy, round face of someone hardy yet huggable. Broad of shoulder, he looked like he could just as easily squeeze a confession out of a hardened soul as soft-pedal a plea for repentance. He became our first genuine celebrity pope, an accomplished communicator and arbiter, and a sportsman to boot.

His work as a young outdoorsy priest at retreats and camps had made him immensely popular with teens. They regarded him as a companion and confidante, albeit an uncompromising rebuker with a touch of compassion. This man of the cloth was decades ahead of his time in connecting, sixties-style, with youth. Yet, while he was comfortable in groups and even among crowds, he often would go off by himself to fervently pray on his own, finding his makeshift sanctuary perhaps fifty or a hundred yards away from the rest. Not especially gregarious or chummy, he was nonetheless approachable and sociable.

What an interesting guy—a survivor, too. He speaks seven languages, narrowly escaped death when Nazis stormed through Poland, proved himself a gifted stage thespian before becoming a priest, was an adept hand at canoes, campfires, and, later as a cardinal, at Vatican councils, and he grittily survived and recovered from a would-be assassin's bullet. He's a poet, too. A pope for all seasons, a compelling figure for a lot of reasons.

As pope, John Paul II has never seen his role as being one to placate, to let sin off the hook with rationalizations and compromise. His stances, e.g., homosexuality as sin and abortion as evil, have at times been as unpopular as he is popular. One thing that he champions more than people is obedience to the Scripture, certainly New Testament as much as Old. In so many ways, he has said that while God rules over all, it is only through professed faith in Jesus Christ as Savior that those calling themselves Christians can spend eternity in heaven.

John Paul II is born-again Christian as much as he is pope. Where many so-called believers choose to play it safe and speak only, or mostly, of God as the sole center of their beliefs—so as not to offend—John Paul has been bold about his frequent reference to Jesus Christ. There is a difference, and the latter suggests a willingness to uphold New Testament tenets in a Christian world often content to pick and choose in making the New Testament "safe" for them.

In *Quotable John Paul II*, we get the full gamut of his views on almost everything, from discipleship, evangelization, and morality to prayer, spirituality, and solidarity—all sourced from much more than just the quarter-century he has served as pope. This book is the essence of this historic man of God, offering his most compelling and sometimes controversial view on dozens of subjects. It is a primer for the Catholic faith and an indispensable record of what made Pope John Paul II the best-known pope in modern times.

AMERICA

1. America, throw open your doors to Christ! Let the seed planted five centuries ago make all areas of your life fruitful: individuals and families, culture and work, economics and politics, the present and future.

2. America faces a . . . time of trial today. Today, the conflict is between a culture that affirms, cherishes, and celebrates the gift of life, and a culture that seeks to declare entire groups of human beings—the unborn, the terminally ill, the handicapped, and others considered "unuseful"—to be outside the boundaries of legal protection.

3. The American separation of church and state as institutions was accompanied from the beginning of your Republic by the conviction that strong religious faith, and the public expression of religiously informed judgments, contribute significantly to the moral health of the body politic.

4.

America
needs much
prayer—lest it
lose its soul.

5. Are you aware of how politically interested the Americans are? Are you aware they are always out to get what they want? Always trying to fulfill their goals?

BUDDHISM

6. Buddhism is in large measure an "atheistic" system.

BUSINESS

7. The purpose of a business firm is not simply to make a profit, but is to be found in its very existence as a community of persons who in various ways are endeavoring to satisfy their basic needs, and who form a particular group at the service of the whole of society.

CHILDREN

8. Children are not a burden on society; they are not a means of profit or people without rights. Children are precious members of the human family, for they embody its hope, its expectations, and its potential.

9. Little children very soon learn about life. They watch and imitate the behavior of adults. They rapidly learn love and respect for others, but they also quickly absorb the poison of violence and hatred. Family experiences strongly condition the attitudes which children will assume as adults.

10. A child's greatest poverty is to be deprived of the love, protection, and tender warmth of a family.

CHRISTMAS

11. One of the popular expressions of the joyful expectation of Christmas is the preparation of the nativity scene in families. In Christian homes these days a special corner is found to display the statuettes, leaving space, between Mary and Joseph, for the Child.

THE CHURCH

12. The service of man is the path of the Church.

13. As the community of all the baptized, the Church is likewise the place of forgiveness, peace, and reconciliation, opening her arms to all people so that she might proclaim to them the true God.

14. Indeed the Church preserves a truth, a doctrine, a wisdom, and an experience which people need if they are to follow the path of true liberation and to reach authentic goodness.

15. The Church is not perfect.

16. The Church cannot be isolated inside its temples, just as men's consciences cannot be isolated from God.

17. Dissent from Church doctrine remains what it is: dissent. As such it may not be proposed or received on an equal footing with the Church's authentic teaching.
    —*rebuking Catholics, clergy included, for picking and choosing which rules to obey and which to ignore*

18. The Church counters the culture of death with the culture of love.

19. The Church is not a political party nor is she identified with any political party; she is above them, open to all people of good will, and no political party can claim the right to represent her.

20. It is not the Church's role to lecture unbelievers. . . . Let us avoid moralizing or suggesting that we have a monopoly on the truth.

COMMUNISM

21. I apologize, but I have lived in Poland, and Communists treat Poles like animals.

      —*responding in 1964 to a suggestion that Catholic teachers be required to take a course in Marxism*

22. I didn't cause this to happen. The tree was already rotten. I just gave it a good shake, and the rotten apple fell.

      —*on the fall of Communism*

COMPASSION

23. In the Old Testament, the Torah teaches that strangers and the homeless in general, inasmuch as they are exposed to all sorts of dangers, deserve special concern from the believer.

DEMOCRACY

24. Democracy is our best opportunity to promote the values that will make the world a better place for everyone, but a society which exalts individual choice as the ultimate source of truth undermines the very foundations of democracy.

25. Democracy is itself a moral adventure, a continuing test of a people's capacity to govern themselves in ways that serve the common good and the good of individual citizens.

DISCIPLESHIP

26. Christians are always in training.

27. Today it is urgently necessary for those who want to be his disciples to drink constantly at the fountains of his gospel in order to proclaim him without compromise.

28. May priests not lose heart and may they reach out to people in order to proclaim the gospel and make disciples of them all!

29. By conforming your daily life to the gospel of the one Teacher who has "the words of eternal life," you will be able to become genuine workers for justice, following the commandment which makes love the new "frontier" of Christian witness.

DIVORCE

30. I have been amazed that all the churches have not made divorce the leading social evil of our day.

31. The Church, which was set up to lead to salvation all people and especially the baptized, cannot abandon to their own devices those who have been previously bound by sacramental marriage and who have attempted a second marriage.

32. The divorced and remarried are and remain her members, because they have received baptism and retain their Christian faith. Of course, a new union after divorce is a moral disorder, which is opposed to precise requirements deriving from the faith, but this must not preclude a commitment to prayer and to the active witness of charity.

ETERNITY

33. If eternity is our horizon as people starving for truth and thirsting for happiness, history is the setting of our daily commitment. Faith teaches us that man's destiny is written in the heart and mind of God, who directs the course of history.

34. Things eternal, things of God, are very simple and very profound.

35. Both the first and second comings have already taken place. We live, however, in expectation of the third coming of Christ, in which creation and redemption will find their definitive fulfillment.

36. People of our time have become insensitive to the Last Things.

—referring to the question of eternal life as it relates to heaven, hell, and purgatory

37.

We want to know if death will be the definitive end of our life or if there is something beyond—if it is possible to hope for an afterlife or not.

EVANGELISM

38. Do not tire, dear brothers and sisters, of working for the renewal of society through effective witness, explicit proclamation, and enlightened attention to the signs of the times.

39. Those who practice charity carry out a profound work of evangelization.

40. It is impossible to address those who are outside the Church, those who attack her, those who do not believe in God, in the same language as those she considers as her faithful.

41. We cannot preach conversion unless we ourselves are converted anew each day.

42. Every generation, with its own mentality and characteristics, is like a new continent to be won for Christ.

Karol Wojtyla at age twelve, in Wadowice, Poland.
(AP/Wide World Photos)

43. The power of evangelization will find itself considerably reduced if those who proclaim the gospel are divided among themselves in all sorts of ways. Is this not perhaps one of the great sicknesses of evangelization today?

44. Every Christian is called to become a strong athlete of Christ, that is, a faithful and courageous witness to his gospel. But to succeed in this, he must persevere in prayer, be trained in virtue, and follow the divine Master in everything.

45. Christians must feel compelled to take the initiative and to reach out to their brothers and sisters in their homes, in the neighborhood, and in the places where they live and work: wherever it is possible to listen together to the one word of salvation—the Word of God—which is more indispensable than bread for everyone's life.

EVIL

46. The truth about man is that he commits evil, that he is a sinner.

47. Temptation is nothing else but directing toward evil everything which man can and ought to put to good use.

48. The history of the twentieth century is a grim warning of the evils that result when human beings are reduced to the status of object to be manipulated by the powerful for selfish gain or for ideological reasons.

49. The gates of hell will not prevail, as the Lord has said. But that doesn't mean we are exempt from the trials from and battles against the Evil One.

FAITH

50. It is faith which stirs reason to move beyond all isolation and willingly to run risks so that it may attain whatever is beautiful, good, and true. Faith thus becomes the convinced and convincing advocate of reason.

51. Do not abandon yourselves to despair. We are the Easter people and hallelujah is our song.

52. There is thus no reason for competition of any kind between reason and faith: each contains the other, and each has its own scope for action.

53. Faith sharpens the inner eye, opening the mind to discover in the flux of events the workings of Providence.

54. Faith can give a human face to the most violent of deaths and show its beauty even in the midst of the most atrocious persecutions.

55. Faith is always demanding, because faith leads us beyond ourselves.

56. Through faith, man achieves the good of his rational nature.

FAMILY

57. The home is the place of family communion, where from the love of husband and wife children are born and learn how to live; in the home children learn those fundamental moral and spiritual values which will make them the citizens and Christians of tomorrow.

58. The family, the great workshop of love, is the first school, indeed a lasting school where people are not taught to love with barren ideas, but with the incisive power of experience.

59. Only by praying together with the children can a father and mother—exercising their royal priesthood—penetrate the innermost depths of their children's hearts and leave an impression that the future events in their lives will not be able to efface.

60. The family is a mystery of love, because it collaborates directly in the creative work of God.

61. Your families must be sanctuaries of love in the midst of the many difficult situations caused by the misuse of God's gift of sexuality.

62. Parents therefore have a right to expect from their sons and daughters the mature fruits of their efforts, just as children and young people have the right to expect from their parents the love and care which leads to a healthy development. All that is the Fourth Commandment.

63. As the family goes, so goes the nation!

64. The family today is threatened not only by external factors, such as social mobility and the new characteristics of work organization, but first and foremost by an individualistic culture without solid ethical moorings, which misinterprets the very meaning of conjugal love and, challenging the co-natural need for stability, undermines the family unit's capacity for lasting communion and peace.

65. Another feature of the cultural context in which we live is the tendency of many parents to renounce their role in order to be merely friends to their children, refraining from warning and correcting them even when this is necessary for teaching them the truth, albeit with every affection and tenderness.

66. To maintain a joyful family requires much from both the parents and the children. Each member of the family has to become, in a special way, the servant of the others.

FATHERHOOD

67. In today's family the father figure is in danger of becoming more and more hidden or even absent.

FELLOWSHIP

68. New ways and structures must be found to build bridges between people, so that there really is that experience of mutual acceptance and closeness which Christian fellowship requires.

FORGIVENESS

69. We should always forgive, remembering that we, too, are in need of forgiveness.

70. Certainly, forgiveness does not come spontaneously or naturally to people. Forgiving from the heart can sometimes be actually heroic.

71. Christ is at the same time both merciful and intransigent. He calls good and evil by their names, without any discussion or compromise; but he also shows himself always ready to forgive.

72. In the context of Christmas and the Holy Year of Redemption, I was able to meet with the person that you all know by name, Ali Agca, who in the year 1981 on the 13th of May made an attempt on my life. But Providence took things in its own hands, in what I would call an extraordinary way, so that today I was able to meet my assailant and repeat to him the pardon I gave him immediately.

FREEDOM

73. Freedom is not simply the absence of tyranny or oppression. Nor is freedom the license to do whatever we like. Freedom has an inner "logic" which distinguishes it and ennobles it.

74. When the noisy propaganda of liberalism grows stronger in our country, too, the shepherds of the Church cannot fail to proclaim the one fail-proof philosophy of freedom, which is the truth of the cross of Christ.

—*speaking in Poland, in 2002*

75. When freedom does not have a purpose, when it does not wish to know anything about the rule of law engraved in the hearts of men and women, when it does not listen to the voice of conscience, it turns against humanity and society.

76. Freedom consists not in doing what we like, but in having the right to do what we ought.

77. Only by admitting his innate dependence can man live and use his freedom to the full, and at the same time respect the freedom of every other person.

78. Freedom needs to be guided by a well-trained conscience which is able both to distinguish between moral good and evil, and to choose good in every situation.

GOD

79. As the source of love, God desires to make himself known; and the knowledge which the human being has of God perfects all that the human mind can know of the meaning of life.

80. We begin with the impression that it's our initiative, but it's always God's initiative within us.

81. Although God allows suffering to exist in the world, He does not enjoy it.

82. God therefore entered the world and human history and proceeds silently, waiting patiently for humanity with its delays and conditioning. He respects its freedom, supports it when it is gripped by desperation, leads it step by step, and invites it to collaborate on the project of truth, justice, and peace of the kingdom. Divine action and human effort must therefore be intertwined.

83. God is faithful even when man, instead of responding with love to God's love, opposes him and treats him like a rival, deluding himself and relying on his own power, with the resulting break of relationship with the one who created him.

84. Neither negating our personality nor depriving us of freedom, God saves us in a way which surpasses all our plans and expectations.

85. People need signs and reminders of God in the modern secular city, which has few reminders of God left.

86. God can penetrate the minds of men in the most unpromising situations, and in spite of systems and regimes which deny his existence.

87. By the authority of his absolute transcendence, God who makes himself known, is also the source of the credibility of what He reveals.

88. Without familiarity with God there is in the last end no consolation in death.

89. God calls everyone to holiness, but without forcing anyone's hand.

THE GOSPEL

90. The gospel is certainly demanding.

91. We must not tamper with God's Word. We must strive to apply the Good News to the ever-changing conditions of the world, but, courageously and at all costs, we must resist the temptation to alter its content or reinterpret it in order to make it fit the spirit of the present age.

92. The fact is that the proclamation of the gospel and human advancement cannot be dissociated.

A shirtless Karol, third from left, at age nineteen, while working construction at a military camp in July 1939. (Adam Gatty-Kostyal photo, AP/Wide World Photos)

93.

The Word of God
transforms the
lives of those who
accept it, because
it is the rule of
faith and action.

94. The Word of God reveals the final destiny of men and women and provides a unifying explanation of all that they do in the world.

GOVERNMENT

95. Governments and their leaders cannot carry on the affairs of state independent of the wishes of their people.

GRACE

96. Only faith can give us certainty that at that moment every sin is forgiven and blotted out by the mysterious intervention of the Savior.

97. The sacrament of Penitence—a conformation to the dead and risen Jesus—also entails the restoration of the supernatural life of grace, or its increase in the case of venial sins. Therefore, the mystery of this sacrament can be fully understood only in relation to the parable of the Prodigal Son.

HAPPINESS

98. True happiness lies in giving ourselves in love to our brothers and sisters.

99. There are no shortcuts to happiness and light.

100. Moral permissiveness does not make man happy.

101.

Happiness
is achieved
through
sacrifice.

HOLINESS

102. Holiness is the fullness of life which Christ offers: he has come that we "may have life, and have it abundantly" (John 10:10).

103. May the Father, who anointed his Son Jesus with the oil of gladness (Heb. 1:5-14), make the heads of each of you shine with the oil of holiness.

HOLY SPIRIT

104. Unity must be the result of a true conversion of everyone, the result of mutual forgiveness, of theological dialogue and fraternal relations, of prayer and of complete docility to the action of the Holy Spirit, who is also the spirit of reconciliation.

105. Through the Spirit, God comes intimately to the person and penetrates the human world more and more.

106. The Holy Spirit reestablishes in the human heart full harmony with God and, assuring man of victory over the Evil One, opens him to the boundless measure of divine love. Thus the Spirit draws man from love of self to love of the Trinity, leading him into the experience of inner freedom and peace, and prompting him to make his own life a gift.

107. When temptation sets its trap and human strength grows weak, then is the moment to invoke the Spirit more urgently, that he (will) come to help us in our weakness and grant us the strength and prudence which God wills.

HOMOSEXUALITY

108. An intrinsic social evil.

109. We can also see how incongruous is the demand
     to accord "marital" status to unions between
     persons of the same sex. It is opposed, first of all,
     by the objective impossibility of making the
     partnership fruitful through the transmission of
     life according to the plan inscribed by God in the
     very structure of the human being. Another
     obstacle is the absence of the conditions for that
     interpersonal complementarity between male and
     female willed by the Creator at both the physical-
     biological and the eminently psychological levels.
     It is only in the union of two sexually different
     persons that the individual can achieve perfection
     in a synthesis of unity and mutual psychophysical
     completion. From this perspective, love is not an
     end in itself and cannot be reduced to the
     corporal joining of two beings, but is a deep
     interpersonal relationship which reaches its
     culmination in total mutual self-giving and in
     cooperation with God the Creator, the ultimate
     source of every new human life.

110. "De facto unions" between homosexuals are a deplorable distortion of what should be a communion of love and life between a man and a woman in a reciprocal gift open to life.

HOPE

111. We must not be afraid of the future.

HUMAN RIGHTS

112. Only the effective protection of the fullness of rights for every individual without discrimination can guarantee peace down to its very foundations.

113. The dignity of the person is the indestructible property of every human being.

114. Human rights cannot be given in the form of concessions. Man is born with them and seeks to realize them in the course of his life.

HUMANITY

115. No man is an iceberg drifting on the ocean of history. Each one of us belongs to a great family, in which he has his own place and his own role to play.

116. Different cultures are, basically, different ways of facing the meaning of personal existence.

117. It is my prayer that scientists will never forget that the cause of humanity is authentically served only if knowledge is joined to conscience.

118. God, from the beginning, established an alliance with man, and with man alone.

119. Man is by nature capable of rising above instinct in his actions.

HUMILITY

120. One of the temptations of our day is that people can become too secure and self-sufficient, and do not have their minds and hearts open to the Word of God.

121. Contemporary man seems to find it harder than ever to recognize his own mistakes and to decide to retrace his steps and begin again after changing course. He seems very reluctant to say "I repent" or "I am sorry."

ISLAM

122. In Islam all the richness of God's self-revelation, which constitutes the heritage of the Old and New testaments, has definitely been set aside.

123. Did you ever read the Qur'an (Koran)? I recommend it. What the Qur'an teaches people is aggression; and what we (Christians) teach our people is peace. . . . Christianity aspires to peace and love. Islam is a religion that attacks. If you start teaching aggression to the whole community, you end up pandering to the negative elements in everyone. You know what that leads to: Such people will assault us.

    —speaking in the early 1990s

124. There is a mystery here, and God will enlighten us about it one day, I am sure.

    —on some fundamental differences
    between Christians and Muslims

125. Islam is not a religion of redemption. There is no room for the cross and resurrection. Jesus is mentioned, but only as a prophet who prepares for the last prophet, Muhammad. . . . For this reason, not only the theology but the anthropology of Islam is very distant from Christianity.

JESUS CHRIST

126. (Christ) is the eternal witness to the Father and to the love that the Father has had for His creatures from the beginning.

127. Everyone's life and the whole of one's life must be at Christ's disposal.

128. The same Jesus who is "the way, the truth and the life" is also "the light of the world"—the light that illumines our path, the light that enables us to perceive the truth, the light of the Son who gives us supernatural life here and hereafter.

129. For the believer, daily effort is a way of preparing for Christ's coming.

130. The hands which broke bread for the disciples at the Last Supper were to be stretched out on the Cross in order to gather all people to himself in the eternal Kingdom of his Father. Through the celebration of the Eucharist, he never ceases to draw men and women to be effective members of his Body.

131. Christ comes into the hearts of our brothers and sisters and visits their consciences. How the image of each and every one changes, when we become aware of this reality, when we make it the subject of our reflections!

132. Despite some common aspects, Christ does not resemble Muhammad or Socrates or Buddha. He is totally original and unique.

133. Jesus asks you not to be ashamed of him and to commit yourselves to proclaiming him to your peers.

134. By knowing the gospel, you will encounter Christ— and do not be afraid of what He may ask of you.

135. Christ cannot be kept out of the history of man in any part of the globe, at any longitude or latitude.

136. Our hearts are anxious. Christ knows our anguish best of all.

137. When you wonder about the mystery of yourself, look to Christ, who gives you the meaning of life. When you wonder what it means to be a mature person, look to Christ, who is the fulfillness of humanity. And when you wonder about your role in the future of the world, look to Christ.

138.

Farmers everywhere provide bread for all humanity, but it is Christ alone who is the bread of life.

Cardinal Karol Wojtyla, Archbishop of Krakow, in 1968. (AP/Wide World Photos)

JUDAISM

139. Once again, through myself, the Church, in the words of the well-known declaration Nostra Aetate, "deplores the hatred, persecutions and displays of anti-Semitism directed against the Jews at any time and by anyone." I repeat, "By anyone."

140. Our elder brothers in the faith.

—*on Jews*

141. Jesus was and always remained a Jew. . . . fully a man of his environment.

KNOWLEDGE

142. From Copernicus to Mendel, from Albert the Great to Pascal, from Galileo to Marconi, the history of the Church and the history of the sciences clearly show us that there is a scientific culture rooted in Christianity. It can be said, in fact, that research, by exploring the greatest and the smallest, contributes to the glory of God which is reflected in every part of the universe.

143. Full spiritual development of a human person is the result of education.

144. Fresh knowledge leads to recognition of the theory of evolution as more than just a hypothesis.

     —acknowledging, in 1996, his opinion of a world in which Darwinian theory and Genesis could coexist

145. God gave you intelligence to know the truth, and your will to achieve what is morally good.

146. Responsibility is not only knowledge. It comes into being at the point where knowledge passes to action.

147. Devote all your energies to developing a culture and a scientific approach which will always let God's providential presence and intervention be disclosed.

     —speaking to scientists

LIFE

148. Our whole life must be a purifying preparation for our encounter with God; tomorrow in eternity, but also today in the Eucharist.

149. The Church today feels the historical need to protect life for the good of man and of civilization.

150. There is no better word than life to sum up comprehensively the greatest aspiration of all humanity.

151. Old age is the crown of the steps of life.

LOVE

152. God loves you all, without distinction, without limit.

153. The ability to love authentically, not great intellectual capacity, constitutes the deepest part of a personality.

154. The love of God is so great that it goes beyond the limits of human language, beyond the grasp of artistic expression, beyond human understanding.

155. Love consists of a commitment which limits one's freedom—it is a giving of the self.

156. What is most essential to love is affirmation of the value of the person.

157. Love is exclusively the portion of human persons.

158. Jesus says that we can enter the kingdom of God only by practicing the commandment of love. We do not enter it, then, through racial, cultural, or religious privileges, but indeed by doing the will of the Father, who is in heaven.

159. The belief that a human being is a person leads to the acceptance of the postulate that enjoyment must be subordinate to love.

MARRIAGE

160. The fact that man "created as man and woman" is the image of God means not only that each of them individually is like God as a rational and free being. It also means that man and woman, created as a "unity of the two" in their common humanity, are called to live in a communion of love and in this way to mirror in the world the communion of love that is in God, through which the three Persons love each other in the intimate mystery of the one divine life.

161. The spouses' Christian love has its example in Christ, who gives Himself completely to the Church and is inscribed in the Paschal Mystery of death and resurrection, of loving sacrifice, of joy and hope.

162. The fear of making permanent commitments can change the mutual love of husband and wife into two loves of self—two loves existing side by side, until they end in separation.

163. Even when difficulties arise, the solution is not flight, nor the breaking of the marriage, but rather the perseverance of the spouses.

164. Marriage has the structure of a covenant, the same covenant by which God entrusted himself to man, expecting in return an analogous confidence in faith.

165. Christ gives to each couple the grace to overcome all obstacles to a lifelong and exclusive union in love.

MEDIA

166. Media products are seen as in some way representing values that the West holds dear and, by implication, they supposedly present Christian values. The truth of the matter may well be that the foremost value they genuinely represent is commercial profit.

167. It is not easy to remain optimistic about the positive influence of the mass media when they appear either to ignore the vital role of religion in the people's lives, or when the treatment that religious belief receives seems consistently negative and unsympathetic.

MERCY

168. I call on Mercy.
—his stated prayer for the world, published in 1982

169. In the Psalms and in the preaching of the prophets, the name "merciful" is perhaps the one most often given to the Lord, in contrast to the persistent cliche whereby the God of the Old Testament is presented above all as severe and vengeful.

170. Christ came not to condemn but to forgive, to show mercy.

171. Mercy is the forgiveness which he never refuses us, as he did not refuse it to Peter after his betrayal.

172. The flowering of the gift of mercy offers liberation from the slavery of evil and gives the strength to sin no more.

MORALITY

173. Obedience to God's Commandments, far from alienating us from our humanity, is the pathway to genuine liberation and the source of true happiness.

174. We must convince ourselves of the priority of the ethical over the technical, of the person over things, of the . . . spiritual over the material.

175. The man who chooses virginity chooses God.

176. Morality is just a measure of humanity. Man fulfills himself in it and through it when he does good. When he performs evils, he destroys the order of morality within himself as well as in the interpersonal and social aspect of his existence.

177. An excuse is worse and more terrible than a lie, for an excuse is a lie guarded.

178. The Church asks those who live in abundance to avoid spiritual blindness, to resist with all their strength the temptation of the power of money.

179. Those who try to live according to the moral law often feel pressured by forces which contradict the things they know in their hearts to be true. And those responsible for teaching moral truth may feel as if their task is virtually impossible, given the power of those external cultural pressures.

180. Conscience is that inner place where "man detects a law which he does not impose upon himself, but which holds him to obedience."

MOTHER MARY

181. May Mary most holy come to the aid of couples in crisis, helping them to rediscover the freshness of their first love.

182. May the Blessed Virgin, who bore him in her womb and contemplated him as she clasped him tightly in her arms, grant us a little of her faith, so that Christ's coming does not leave our lives untouched and our hearts cold.

183. When we turn to Mary our hope is revived. Indeed, she is a part of our humanity, and in her we contemplate the glory God promises to those who respond to his call.

MOTHER TERESA

184. It was providential that Mother Teresa died at the same time as (Princess) Diana.

185. She was a great and appreciated teacher of life, especially for young people, whom she reminded that their great task is to build peace, starting with their families, and to defend life always and everywhere, especially when it is particularly weak. May her witness be an incentive and an encouragement for many young men and women to put themselves generously at the service of the gospel.

MOTHERHOOD

186. Motherhood shows a creativity on which the humanity of each human being largely depends; it also invites man to learn and to express his own fatherhood. Thus women contribute to society and to the Church their ability to nurture human beings.

187. Women as mothers have an irreplaceable role.

THE PAPACY

188. You're crazy.

—his response in 1974 to a professor's proclamation that someday he would be pope

189. What are we going to do with this Polish pope, this Slavic pope? What can we do?

—joking, rhetorically, while giving a homily in Poland early in his papacy

190.

I think that God raised me to be pope, to do something for the world. I have to do something for the good of the world, and for Poland.

191. I still have to learn how to behave like a pope.
> *—joking to onlookers after forgetting to give a papal blessing at a public appearance during the first month of his pontificate*

192. I'm the pope, and I know how to behave.
> *—rebuking a prelate who tried to caution the pope about speaking too long in public*

193. They told my predecessor what he should do and when, and this may have led to his early death. They will not tell me what to do or when. I will decide. They will not kill me.
> *—confiding to a friend early in his pontificate*

194. How can the pope live to be a hundred when you shout him down? Will you let me speak?
> *—jokingly addressing tens of thousands of overly exuberant Polish youths*

PEACE

195. Peace bears the name of Jesus Christ.

*Pope John Paul II prays before the Death Wall memorial to concentration
camp victims, at Auschwitz, Poland, in June 1979.
(AP/Wide World Photos)*

196. I am now willing to recognize that we others, Catholics, have not always been the builders of peace.

197. Peace is a gift of God; but men and women must first accept this gift in order to build a peaceful world. People can do this only if they have a childlike simplicity of heart.

PENANCE

198. The practice of the virtue of penance and the sacrament of Penance are essential for sustaining in us and continually deepening that spirit of veneration which man owes to God himself and to his love so marvelously revealed.

199. Penance also means changing one's life in harmony with the change of heart, and in this sense doing penance is completed by bringing forth fruits worthy of penance.

200. Doing penance is something authentic and effective only if it is translated into deeds and acts of penance.

PERSECUTION

201. In many ages and in many places, Christians have been the object of hatred, persecution, and extermination. They have nevertheless experienced the Redeemer's consoling promise: "Not a hair of your head will be harmed. By patient endurance you will save your lives."

PERSEVERANCE

202. A disabled person, just like every other weak person, must be encouraged to take charge of his own life. It is therefore the task of the family, having overcome the initial shock, to understand first of all that the value of life transcends that of efficiency.

203. The way Jesus shows you is not easy. Rather, it is like a path winding up a mountain. Do not lose heart! The steeper the road, the faster it rises toward ever wider horizons.

PHILOSOPHY

204. One of the major concerns of classical philosophy was to purify human notions of God of mythological elements. We know that Greek religion, like most cosmic religions, was polytheistic, even to the point of divinizing natural things and phenomena.

205. All men and women, as I have noted, are in some sense philosophers and have their own philosophical conceptions with which they direct their lives.

206. The Church considers philosophy an indispensable help for a deeper understanding of faith and for communicating the truth of the gospel to those who do not yet know it.

207. Philosophy moreover is the mirror which reflects the culture of a people.

POLAND

208. [I kiss the soil] as if I placed a kiss on the hands of a mother, for the homeland is our earthly mother. I consider it my duty to be with my compatriots in this sublime and difficult moment.

209. I say, you are telling me to desert Rome!

> *—a teary-eyed response at an August 2002 farewell Mass in Krakow to two million Poles shouting to him their love and pleas to stay*

210. God bless you. I would like to add "until next time," but this is entirely in God's hands.

> *--upon leaving Poland in August 2002 as an ailing 82-year-old pope having made his ninth papacy visit to his home country*

POLITICS

211. Political power falls by right to political communities; the Church, a community established by Christ, does not aspire to such power.

POWER

212.

Power is responsibility: It is service, not privilege.

PRAYER

213. Prayer represents an enormous spiritual power.

214. Prayer enables us to meet God at the most profound level of our being.

215. The Lord refreshes and satisfies the person who prays, making him share in his fullness of immortal life.

216. Above all, you must pray without ceasing for your priests, that the gift of God which they have received through the laying on of hands may be constantly rekindled.

217. In the silence of prayer, encounter with God is actuated.

218. Prayer fills the mind with truth and gives hope to the heart.

219. My father was the person who explained to me the mystery of God and made me understand. Even now, when I awake at night, I remember seeing my father kneeling, praying.

220. When a man goes down on his knees in a confessional because he has sinned, at that very moment he adds to his own dignity as a man.

221. Wherever people are praying in the world, there the Holy Spirit is, the living breath of prayer.

222. Prayer always remains the voice of all those who apparently have no voice.

PRIESTHOOD

223. Watchful and vigilant, the pastor looks on his
faithful and on the whole of society in the light of
the gospel and of his ecclesial experience.

224. You are priests, not social or political leaders. Let
us not be under the illusion that we are serving
the gospel through an exaggerated interest in the
wide field of temporal problems.

225. All those who have received the grace of the
priesthood are made stewards of God's mysteries
through the proclamation of the Word, the
celebration of the sacraments, and the loving
guidance of the Christian community.

226. The vow of celibacy is a matter of keeping one's
word to Christ and the Church, a duty and a
proof of the priest's inner maturity; it is the
expression of his personal dignity.

227.

The gospel demands that bishops should deal promptly, frankly, and resolutely with any situation which scandalizes the flock or weakens the credibility of the Church's witness. Following the example of Christ the Good Shepherd, you are to seek out those in difficulty and gently "admonish them as beloved children."

228. In the Church and on behalf of the Church, priests are a sacramental representation of Jesus Christ, the Head and Shepherd.

229. In order to remove any doubt, by virtue of my ministry of confirming the brethren, I declare that the Church has no authority whatsoever to confer priestly ordination on women and that all the faithful are definitively bound to this judgment.

230. The small number of priests means that they are frequently pushed to the limits of their strength.

231. Sunday homilies should therefore be prepared with great care, prayer, and study, as they will help the faithful live their faith in their daily lives and enter into dialogue with their brothers and sisters.

REPENTANCE

232. People cannot come to true and genuine repentance until they realize that sin is contrary to the ethical norm written in their inmost being.

233. Every confessional is a special and blessed place from which, with divisions wiped away, there is born new and uncontaminated a reconciled individual—a reconciled world!

RIGHT TO LIFE

234. The right to life does not depend on a particular religious conviction.

235. A child conceived in its mother's womb is never an unjust aggressor; it is a defenseless being that is waiting to be welcomed and helped.

236. Abortion and euthanasia—the actual killing of another human being—are hailed as rights and solutions to problems. The slaughter of the innocents is no less sinful or devastating simply because it is done in a legal and scientific way. In the modern metropolis, life—God's first gift and the fundamental right for every individual on which all other rights are based—is often treated as just one more commodity to be organized, commercialized, and manipulated according to convenience.

-—*speaking in Denver*

237. The life of the fetus must be protected, defended, and nurtured in the mother's womb because of its inherent dignity, a dignity which belongs to the embryo and is not something conferred or granted by others, whether the genetic parents, the medical personnel, or the state.

238. The Church intends not only to reaffirm the right
      to life—the violation of which is an offense against
      the human person and against God the Creator
      and Father, the loving source of all life—but she
      also intends to devote herself ever more fully to
      concrete defense and promotion of this right.

239. Procured abortion is the deliberate and direct
      killing, by whatever means it is carried out, of a
      human being in the initial phase of his or her
      existence.

ROOTS

240. Fidelity to roots does not mean a mechanical
      copying of the past. Fidelity to roots is always
      creative.

THE SABBATH

241. Unfortunately, when Sunday loses its fundamental meaning and becomes merely part of a "weekend," it can happen that people stay locked within a horizon so limited that they can no longer see "the heavens." Hence, though ready to celebrate, they are really incapable of doing so.

242. I would strongly urge everyone to rediscover Sunday: Do not be afraid to give your time to Christ! Yes, let us open our time to Christ, that he may cast light upon it and give it direction.

243. Sunday is the day of rest because it is the day "blessed" by God and "made holy" by him, set apart from the other days to be, among all of them, "the Lord's Day."

244.

Through Sunday
rest, daily
concerns and
tasks can find
their proper
perspective.

SACRIFICE

245. The sacrifice of Isaac anticipates that of Christ: the Father did not spare his own Son, but gave him up for the world's salvation. He who withheld Abraham's arm when he was at the point of immolating Isaac, did not hesitate to sacrifice his own Son for our redemption. Abraham's sacrifice thus emphasizes the fact that human sacrifices must never be performed anywhere, since the only true and perfect sacrifice is that of the only begotten and eternal Son of the living God.

246. After the sacrifice of the Son of God, no further human expiation is necessary since his sacrifice on the cross includes and surpasses all others that man could offer God.

SALVATION

247. Christianity is a religion of salvation.

248. Salvation not only confronts evil in each of its existing forms in this world but proclaims victory over evil.

249. Christ is the true active subject of humanity's salvation.

250. God's salvation is the work of a love greater than man's sin.

SELF

251. Man is called to victory over himself.

252. For many people, especially the young, the city becomes an experience of rootlessness, anonymity, and inequality, with the consequent loss of identity and sense of human dignity. The result is often the violence that now marks so many of the large cities, not least in your own country.

253. Any man who chooses his ideology honestly and through his own conviction deserves respect.

254. The admonition "Know yourself" was carved on the temple portal at Delphi, as testimony to a basic truth to be adopted as a minimal norm by those who seek to set themselves apart from the rest of creation as "human beings," that is as those who "know themselves."

Celebrating an open-air Easter Mass in April 1981 at Saint Peter's Square, in front of about 200,000 people.
(AP/Wide World Photos)

SEXUALITY

255. Sex not only decides the physical individuality of
     man, but at the same time defines his personal
     identity.

THE SICK

256. Whoever suffers from mental illness always bears
     God's image and likeness in himself, as does every
     human being.

257. Our Lord Jesus Christ, the Son of God made man,
     loved the sick; he devoted a great part of his
     earthly ministry to healing the sick and
     comforting the afflicted.

258. There was a time when I was afraid to approach
     those who were ill: I felt a sort of remorse when
     confronted with this suffering which I had been
     spared.

259. Christ took all human suffering on himself,
even mental illness. Yes even this affliction,
which perhaps seems the most absurd and
incomprehensible, configures the sick person
to Christ and gives him a share in his
redeeming passion.

SIN

260. Sin is a negation of God as creator in his
relationship to man and of what God wills for
man from the beginning and forever.

261. Contradiction is obliteration of the line of
demarcation between good and evil: It means
calling humanism what is actually "sin."

262. What John the Baptist was conferring on the
banks of the Jordan was a baptism of repentance
for conversion and the forgiveness of sins.

263. The "dungeon" from which the Lord comes to release us is first of all the one where the spirit is chained. Sin is the prison of the spirit.

264. Eden makes us think about the tragic consequences of rejecting the Father, which becomes evident in man's inner disorder and in the breakdown of harmony between man and woman, brother and brother.

265. As a rupture with God, sin is an act of disobedience by a creature who rejects, at least implicitly, the very one from whom he came and who sustains him in life.

266. There is a certain solitude of the sinner in his sin, and this can be seen dramatically represented in Cain with sin "crouching at his door," as the Book of Genesis says so effectively.

267. It is wonderful to be able to confess our sins, and to hear as a balm the word which floods us with mercy and sends us on our way again.

268. Our sin has disrupted God's plan, and its effects are not only felt in human life but also in creation itself. This cosmic dimension of the effects of sin becomes almost tangible in ecological disasters.

269. Sin is devastating. It drives peace from hearts and causes a chain of sufferings in human relationships.

270. I say it to those responsible: Repent! One day you will come face to face with the judgment of God!
    —*speaking out to the Mafia during a 1993 Mass in Sicily*

SOLIDARITY

271. In the name of the future of mankind, this word "solidarity" must be pronounced.
    —*using one of his favorite words*

272. The knowledge that Christ remains among his people encourages believers and spurs them to promote authentic solidarity by actively working to build the "civilization of love."

273. Work properly understood is a service to others. It creates links of solidarity.

274. We need first of all to foster, in ourselves and in others, a contemplative outlook. Such an outlook arises from faith in the God of life.

275. The real challenge facing developing nations is as much spiritual as material.

276. A society or culture which wishes to survive cannot declare the spiritual dimension of the human person to be irrelevant to public life.

SPORTS

277. Sports, in fact, can make an effective contribution to peaceful understanding between peoples and to establishing the new civilization of love.

278. The importance of sports today invites those who participate in them to take this opportunity for an examination of conscience. It is important to identify and promote the many positive aspects of sport, but it is only right also to recognize the various transgressions to which it can succumb.

279. It's a sport that is especially suited to small people. They have less far to fall than tall people!
     —*on skiing, spoken after becoming pope*

280.

That golf, that's a stupid game. Chasing a little white ball all over the grass.

281. The athlete, therefore, agrees with the Psalmist when he says that the effort spent in sowing finds its reward in the joy of the harvest: "Although they go forth weeping, carrying the seed to be sown, they shall come back rejoicing, carrying their sheaves" (Ps. 125:6).

SUFFERING

282. Human suffering is a continent of which none of us can claim to have reached the boundaries.

283. Suffering, in fact, is always a great test not only of physical strength but also of spiritual strength.

284. Pain is a call to love, which means that it ought to engender solidarity, self-giving, generosity in those who suffer and in those called to accompany and aid them in their distress.

TRUST

285. It is impossible to put your trust in another human being, knowing or feeling that his or her sole aim is utility or pleasure.

TRUTH

286. It is the nature of the human being to seek the truth.

287. If freedom does not obey the truth, it can crush you.

288. Recent times have seen the rise to prominence of various doctrines which tend to devalue even the truths which had been judged certain.

289. Freedom of conscience is never freedom from the truth but always and only freedom in the truth.

290. A real scholar never sees himself as superior to other men, but as a servant of the truth.

291. There are three truths about every human being. A historical truth—that is the easiest, because you can investigate it. The second one is a psychological truth—the conscience; the only one who knows it is the person himself. And the third truth is the normative truth—truth in reference to moral rules.

292. You cannot take a vote on the truth.
   —*addressing an American journalist*

VIOLENCE

293. Social justice cannot be attained by violence. Violence kills what it intends to create.

294. Whenever violence is done in the name of religion, we must make it clear to everyone that in such instances, we are not dealing with true religion.

VOCATION

295. My vocation has always been mainly active in character.

WAR

296. Apart from being immoral, war today is useless and harmful.

297. War is evil. It should be avoided even as a last resort to restore justice between countries, because it may result in even greater evil and injustice than it combats.

WOMEN

298. Both man and woman are human beings to an equal degree, both are created in God's image.

299. In God's eternal plan, woman is the one in whom the order of love in the created world of person first takes root.

300. Certainly much remains to be done to prevent discrimination against those who have chosen to be wives and mothers.

301. How many women have been and are still valued more for their physical appearance than for their personal qualities, professional competence, intellectual work, the richness of their sensitivity, and, finally, for the very dignity of their being!

302. The personal resources of femininity are certainly no less than the resources of masculinity: They are merely different.

303. A certain contemporary feminism finds its roots in the absence of true respect for women.

304. In the name of liberation from male "domination," women must not appropriate to themselves male characteristics contrary to their own feminine "originality."

305.

Women have a
full right to
become actively
involved in all
areas of public
life.

The pope meets with U.S. president Ronald Reagan in Miami in September 1987. (Bob Daugherty photo, AP/Wide World Photos)

WORK

306. With his silent diligence in Joseph's workshop, Jesus gave the highest proof of the dignity of work.

307. In God's plan, work is therefore seen as a right and duty. Necessary to make the earth's resources benefit the life of each person and of society, it helps to direct human activity toward God in the fulfillment of his command to "subdue the earth."

308. I know very well how necessary it is for a person to have work that is not alienating and frustrating, to have work that recognizes his full dignity.

309. Work bears a particular mark of man and of humanity, the mark of a person operating within a community of persons.

310. Since the work that awaits everyone in the vineyard of the Lord is so great, there is no place for idleness.

311. Don't be worried, the hard work kills the time. And it is through work that man more fully becomes man.

> —*Karol, twenty, to a university colleague while both were working in a quarry under brutal conditions*

312. Were it not for human work, there would be no bread and wine. Without bread and wine, there would not be among us the Son of God.

THE WORLD

313. The mere accumulation of goods and services, even for the benefit of the majority, is not enough for the realization of human happiness.

314. Modern society will find no solution to the ecological problem unless it takes a serious look at its lifestyles.

315. Man realizes that this world, with all its many riches, is superficial and precarious; in a sense, it is destined for death.

316. In the modern metropolis, life . . . is often treated as just one more commodity to be organized, commercialized, and manipulated according to convenience.

317. Broad sectors of public opinion justify certain crimes against life in the name of individual freedom, and on this basis they claim not only exemption from punishment but even authorization by the state.

318. While people sometimes speak of periods of "acceleration" in the economic life and civilization of humanity or of individual nations, linking these periods to the progress of science and technology and especially to discoveries which are decisive for social and economic life, at the same time it can be said that none of these phenomena of "acceleration" exceeds the essential content of what was said in that most ancient of biblical tests.

319.

Woe to societies where scandal becomes an everyday event.

320. All over the world people live in constant terror and anxiety. I myself, I the pope, have to be guarded and surrounded by police agents when I cross the streets of Rome to visit a parish. . . . My God! Such a situation should be inconceivable.

—from an essay on terrorism the pope wrote not long before Mehmet Ali Agca's assassination attempt on him

321. Human beings are both child and parent of the culture in which they are immersed.

322. Nature cannot be conquered by violating its laws.

WORSHIP

323. I have a sweet tooth for song and music. This is my Polish sin.

324. Man's social nature itself requires that he give external expression to his internal acts of religion, that he communicate with others in religious matters, and that he profess his religion in community.

325. Sunday is the day when the whole community is called together; this is why it is also called "dies ecclesiae," the day of the Church.

326. Eucharistic worship is therefore precisely the expression of that love which is the authentic and deepest characteristic of the Christian vocation.

327. Religious denominations, in bringing together believers of a given faith, exist and act as social bodies organized according to their own doctrinal principles and institutional purposes.

YOUNG PEOPLE

328. When young people chase after false ideals, they can experience bitterness and humiliation, hostility and hatred, absorbing the discontent and emptiness all around them.

329. I have two responsibilities to youth: canoeing and skiing.

    —referring to his frequent appearances
    at church-sponsored gatherings in the fifties

330. Young people should be helped to discover very early on the value of gift of self, an essential factor in reaching personal maturity.

331. In the young there is, in fact, an immense potential for good and for creative ability.

332. Young people are threatened . . . by the evil use of advertising techniques that stimulate the natural inclination to avoid hard work by promising the immediate satisfaction of every desire.

POPE-POURRI

333. MY LOLEK WILL BECOME A GREAT PERSON.

—*Emilia Wojtyla, his mom*

334. DON'T WORRY; IT'S NOT AS IF YOU WANTED TO BE POPE.

—*a classmate to nine-year-old Karol Wojtyla after the latter had scored a zero on a catechism test*

335. HE WAS ALWAYS RATHER SHY, SOMETIMES A LITTLE AWKWARD, NOT VERY SOCIAL.

—*Jacek Wozniakowski, a friend*

336. KAROL WAS DIFFERENT. AFTER HALF AN HOUR (OF AFTER-SCHOOL PLAY), HE WOULD GO HOME TO STUDY. WHEN I CAME BACK FROM THE PLAYGROUND, I WENT TO HIM TO COPY THE LATIN HOMEWORK HE HAD ALREADY DONE.
—Zbigniew Silkowski, childhood pal

337. After my father's death, I became aware of my true path. I was working at a plant and devoting myself, as far as the terrors of the occupation allowed, to my taste in literature and drama. My priestly vocation took place in the midst of all that—I knew I was called with absolute clarity.
—John Paul II

John Paul II kisses the forehead of a twenty-day-old baby outside Saint Etienne-du-Mont Church in Paris, in August 1997. (Laurent Rebours photo, AP/Wide World Photos)

338. I was spared much of the immense and horrible drama of the Second World War. I could have been arrested any day, at home, in the stone quarry, in the plant, and taken away to a concentration camp. Sometimes I would ask myself: So many young people of my own age are losing their lives, why not me? Today I know that it was not mere chance.

—*John Paul II*

339. HE HAD EVERY OPPORTUNITY TO HAVE THAT
KIND OF RELATIONSHIP IF HE HAD WANTED TO.
BUT HE KNEW HE WAS BEING LED TOWARD
SOMETHING MORE IMPORTANT.

*—an unnamed woman friend, discussing
speculation that, as a youth, the future
Pope John Paul II had had a serious
romantic relationship with a young woman*

340. WE REHEARSED SO MANY ROLES
TOGETHER THAT I CAN SAY IT WITH
ASSURANCE: HE WAS THE BEST. WHEN WE
HEARD THAT HE WAS GOING TO BECOME A
PRIEST, WE ALL DESPAIRED.

*—Danuta Michalowska, an actress with whom he
shared numerous theatrical credits in his youth*

341. The word is the key to dramatic
ferment—a ferment through which
flow the deeds of men and out of which
they draw their dynamism.
    —as a young thespian explaining the state of theater at a
    time when resources for stage decor and scenery were unavailable

342. Listen: the even knocking of hammers,
So much their own
I project onto the people
To test the strength of each blow.
Listen now: electric current
Cuts through a river of rock.
And a thought grows in me day after day:
The greatness of work is inside man.
    —an excerpt from his poem
    "The Quarry," which he wrote at age twenty

343. TODAY, MANY PRIESTS TRY TO BE LIKE THE
KIDS. WE WERE TRYING TO BE LIKE HIM.

*—Stanislaw Rybicki, who as a youth was
one of a thousand boys and girls who spent
time with the future pope in outdoor
settings of worship and evangelization*

344. MOST PEOPLE ARE INTERESTED JUST IN HIS
TEACHING ON SEX. AND SINCE THEY DON'T
LIKE WHAT HE SAYS ABOUT SEX, THEY MISS
WHAT IS IMPORTANT.

—Halina Bortnowska, a friend and former student

345. IT'S NOT AN EASY BOOK. IT DEALS WITH ISSUES
BETWEEN MEN AND WOMEN THAT MANY
PRIESTS WOULD RATHER TRY AND AVOID.

*—Father Bardecki, referring to Wojtyla's bold
and blunt book* Love and Responsibility,
which became a bestseller in Poland in the sixties

346. FOR HIM, THE PRESENCE OF THE HOLY SPIRIT
WAS VERY STRONG FROM THE BEGINNING.
—*Mieczyslaw Malinski, a fellow seminarian*

347. HE IS A COMPLEX FIGURE. THERE'S A PERSONAL
HOLINESS . . . AND A GREAT COURAGE TO
CONFRONT INJUSTICE WHEREVER HE FINDS IT
(AND THERE IS ALSO) DOCTRINAL CONSERVATISM
. . . AND A KIND OF AUTHORITARIAN
CHARACTER TO HIS PERSONALITY.
—*Chester Gillis, Georgetown
University theology professor*

348. YOU CANNOT TAG A LABEL ON HIM. HE'S EVEN
A BIT MISCHIEVOUS. JUST LIKE A CLOSE
MEMBER OF THE FAMILY!
—*a Canadian journalist, describing Cardinal Wojtyla
during a 1969 trip to Canada and the United States*

349.

I am not in a hurry.

—*a young Karol Wojtyla*

350.

I accept.

Where do I

sign?

—Karol's prompt response, at age thirty-eight
in 1958, upon learning that he had been
nominated to become Poland's youngest-ever bishop

351. HE USED SMALL GROUP DISCUSSIONS TO GET EVERYONE INVOLVED, AND HE WOULD MOVE FROM GROUP TO GROUP, LISTENING, COMMENTING, ENCOURAGING THEM. HE HAD THE PROCESS COMPLETELY UNDER CONTROL, BUT HE WASN'T AUTHORITARIAN IN ANY WAY. IT WAS EXCELLENT PREPARATION FOR A FUTURE POPE.

—Stefan Wilkanowicz, a longtime friend and magazine editor, describing Cardinal Wojtyla's knack for conducting meetings and conventions in his Polish archdiocese

352. AND IF A POLISH POPE WERE ELECTED, I WILL BUY YOU ALL CHAMPAGNE.

—a Polish government official, joking to a crowd of journalists less than an hour before the shocking announcement that Karol Wojtyla had been elected the newest pope

353. NOBODY KNEW WHO HE WAS. SOMEONE THOUGHT HE WAS AN ORIENTAL. IT SOUNDED LIKE A CHINESE NAME.

> —*Monsignor Tony Bevilacqua, reacting to Karol Wojtyla's somewhat surprising election as the new pope, in October 1978*

354. HE'LL BE REMEMBERED MORE THAN ANYTHING FOR ARTICULATING COMMUNISM'S BETRAYAL OF HUMAN FREEDOM AND THE INSPIRATION HE GAVE TO THOSE WHO HELPED BRING IT DOWN NONVIOLENTLY.

> —*R. Scott Appleby, University of Notre Dame history professor*

355. THIS KIND OF ACCUSATION WAS NOTHING NEW TO US.

> —*Andrei Gromyko, Soviet foreign minister, referring to a 1979 meeting in which the pope asked Gromyko about reports that the Soviet Union still was blocking freedom of religion*

356.

TAKE MY ADVICE,
DON'T GIVE HIM ANY
RECEPTION. IT WILL CAUSE
TROUBLE . . . . TELL THE
POPE—HE'S A WISE MAN—
HE CAN DECLARE PUBLICLY
THAT HE CAN'T COME DUE
TO ILLNESS.

—*Leonid Brezhnev, Soviet party leader, chastising
Polish party leader Edward Gierek, in 1979, over
the latter's desire to invite the new pope back
for a home-country reception. The visit took place.*

John Paul II rides the "Popemobile" through the streets of Marija Bistrica in Croatia in October 1998. This was on the occasion of his beatifying Cardinal Alojzije Stepinac, a Croatian World War II war hero. (Darko Bandic photo, AP/Wide World Photos)

357. The pope who began his papacy with the words "Be not afraid!" tries to be completely faithful to this exhortation and is always ready to be at the service of man, nations, and humanity in the spirit of this truth of the gospel.

—*John Paul II*

358. EVEN THOUGH IT MAY SOUND CYNICAL, HE, UNLIKE SOME OF HIS PREDECESSORS, I SENSE TRULY BELIEVES IN GOD.

—*Zbigniew Brzezinski*

359. THE POPE IS SAYING THERE OUGHT TO BE A BALANCE, THAT SOCIAL JUSTICE AND MORAL IMPERATIVES OUGHT TO BE VIEWED BY SOCIETY AS VALUES AT LEAST AS IMPORTANT AS CONSUMER SATISFACTION.

—*Brzezinski*

360. HOLY FATHER, I SINCERELY ADMIRE YOUR COURAGEOUS STATEMENTS ON THE EVENTS SURROUNDING GALILEO AND THE INQUISITION'S KNOWN ERRORS, ON THE CRUSADES' BLOODY EPISODES AND THE CRIMES COMMITTED DURING THE CONQUEST OF THE AMERICAS, ALSO ON CERTAIN SCIENTIFIC DISCOVERIES THAT TODAY ARE NOT CONTESTED BY ANYBODY BUT WHICH, IN THEIR TIMES, WERE THE TARGET OF SO MANY PREJUDICES AND ANATHEMAS. THAT CERTAINLY REQUIRED THE IMMENSE AUTHORITY YOU HAVE COME TO ATTAIN WITHIN YOUR CHURCH.

—Fidel Castro, in his statement of welcome upon Pope John Paul II's visit to Cuba in January 1998

361. HE UTTERED NO WORD OF DESPAIR OR
RESENTMENT; SIMPLY WORDS OF PROFOUND
PRAYER SPRINGING FROM GREAT SUFFERING.

—Stanislaw Dziwisz, a monsignor,
recalling the eight-minute trip to
the Gemelli Clinic after the pope was shot

362. Have we said compline?
—the pope's first words after regaining consciousness
the day after the 1981 assassination attempt on his life

363. The human body in history dies more often
and earlier than the tree.

Man endures beyond the doors of death in
catacombs and crypts.

Man who departs endures in those who
follow.

Man who follows endures in those departed.

—from his poem "A Conversation with God"

364. I SPOKE TO HIM IN ITALIAN, BUT HE SAW THIS AS AN OPPORTUNITY TO SPEAK ENGLISH. I CAME IN WITH SIX POINTS AND DIDN'T GET THROUGH TO HIM WITH ANY OF THEM.

> —*Fr. Ted Hesburgh, then Notre Dame University president, referring to a 1979 meeting with the pope that could have been construed as a brush-off*

365. HE CAME HERE LIKE MOSES.

> —*a Pole remarking on a visit to his native Poland by Pope John Paul II*

366. Well, if you had any moonshine—the kind I used to have when I was young—I'd have a glass.

> —*reportedly his answer to bodyguard Roman Holdys' query if he wanted anything to drink while en route by helicopter to visit Polish Solidarity leader Lech Walesa*

367. You will forgive me, ladies and gentlemen, for evoking this memory, but I would be untrue to the history of this century, I would be dishonest with regard to the great cause of man which we all wish to service, if I should keep silence—I who come from the country on whose living body Auschwitz was at one time constructed.

—John Paul II

368. I wish I could be out there now somewhere in the mountains, racing down into a valley. It's an extraordinary sensation.

     —*spoken while wistfully gazing out the window of his office*

369. How did I do? Can I land a job in Hollywood? I studied to be an actor as a young man, you know.

     —*after taping an interview with James Michener for a television special series*

370. WE ARE WITNESSING A MAN GIVING HIMSELF TO THE END. FOR THE FIRST TIME, THE WORLD WILL WATCH A POPE DIE.

     —**George Weigel,** *author of* **Witness to Hope: The Biography of Pope John Paul II**

Notes

1. Bunson, Matthew E., *Papal Wisdom*. New York: Dutton, 1994, p. 146.
2. FDCH Political Transcripts, January 26, 1999.
3. Message to the Fiftieth National Prayer Breakfast, U.S. Congress, February 3, 2000.
4. Pope John Paul II, *Celebrate the Third Millennium: Facing the Future with Hope*. Ann Arbor, MI: Servant Publications, 1999, p. 51 (from letter to the bishops of the United States on the recent scandal given by members of the clergy, June 11, 1993).
5. Kwitny, Jonathan, *Man of the Century: The Life and Times of Pope John Paul II*. New York: Henry Holt and Co., 1997, p. 453.
6. John Paul II, *Crossing the Threshold of Hope*. Translated from Italian by Jenny McPhee and Martha McPhee. New York: Alfred A. Knopf, 1994, p. 86.
7. Kwitny, p. 622.
8. World Day of Peace, January 1, 1996.
9. Ibid.
10. "Disregard of Family Threatens Society," December 12, 1996.
11. "The Lord is Near," Angelus Message, December 12, 1999.
12. Pope John Paul II, edited by Cardinal Achille Silvestrini, *A Pilgrim Pope: Messages for the World*. Kansas City, MO: Andrews McMeel, 1999, p. 299.
13. Ibid., p. 302.
14. "Ad Limina Apostolorum," Bishops Conference of Brazil, 10, October 18, 1995.
15. Frossard, Andrew, and Pope John Paul II (translated from French by J. R. Foster), *Be Not Afraid*. New York, St. Martin's Press, 1984, p. 160.
16. Kwitny, p. 579.
17. Moody, John, *Pope John Paul II. A Biography* book. New York: Park Lane Press, 1997, p. 143.
18. "Ad Limina Apostolorum," Bishops Conference of Brazil, 10, October 18, 1995.
19. Weigel, George, *Witness to Hope: The Biography of Pope John Paul II*. New York: Cliff Street Books, 1999, p. 667.
20. Bernstein, Carl, and Marco Politi, *His Holiness: John Paul II and the Hidden History of Our Time*. New York: Doubleday, 1996, p. 102.
21. Kwitny, p. 196.
22. Bernstein and Politi, p. 356.
23. "Developing Special Concern for the Homeless," Lent 1997 message for the first year of preparation for the Great Jubilee of the Year 2000.
24. Message to the Fiftieth National Prayer Breakfast, U.S. Congress.
25. *Ad Limina* Address to the Bishops of Texas, Oklahoma, and Arkansas, June 6, 1998.
26. Pope John Paul II, *A Pilgrim Pope*, p. 316.

27. "Proclaim the Gospel Without Compromise," May 3, 2000.

28. "*Ad Limina Apostolorum*": Bishops' Conference of France 2.

29. "You Have the Words of Eternal Life," Message to Young People for the 11th World Youth Day, in 1996.

30. Kwitny, p. 495.

31. "Pastoral Care of Divorced and Remarried," to Pontifical Council for the Family, January 24, 1997.

32. Ibid.

33. "You Have the Words of Eternal Life."

34. Hebblethwaite, Peter, and Ludwig Kaufmann, *John Paul II: A Pictorial Biography*. New York: McGraw-Hill, 1979, p. 62.

35. "Watch and Pray for the Lord's Return," Saint Jerome Emiliani Parish, Rome, December 1, 1996.

36. John Paul II, *Crossing the Threshold of Hope*, p. 183.

37. "Fides et Ratio," Encyclical Letter to the Catholic Bishops of the World, September 18, 1998.

38. "Proclaim the Gospel Without Compromise," May 3, 2000.

39. Pope John Paul II, "Celebrate the Third Millennium," p. 141, from address to the pontifical council, *Cor Unum*, April 18, 1997.

40. *John Paul II: Chronicle of a Remarkable Life*. New York: Dorling Kindersley, American edition, 2000, p. 70.

41. Pope John Paul II, edited by Alexandria Hatcher, *Forgiveness: Thoughts for the New Millennium*. Kansas City, MO: Andrews McMeel, 1999, p. 92.

42. Pope John Paul II, A *Pilgrim Pope*, p. 14.

43. Sullivan, Robert, and the editors of *Life, Pope John Paul II: A Tribute*. New York: Time Inc. Home Entertainment, 1999, p. 71.

44. "Jubilee of Sports People," October 29, 2000.

45. Sunday Homily, February 21, 1999.

46. Frossard and Pope John Paul II, p. 80.

47. Pope John Paul II, *Fear Not: Thoughts on Living in Today's World*, p. 14.

48. Ad Limina Address to the Bishops of Texas, Oklahoma, and Arkansas.

49. Bernstein and Politi, p. 430.

50. "Fides et Ratio."

51. BrainyQuote.com

52. "Fides et Ratio."

53. Pope John Paul II, *Celebrate the Third Millennium*, p. 14, from *Fides et Ratio*, September 18, 1998.

54. Ibid., p. 27, from *Incarnationis Mysterium*, Bull of Indictment of the Great Jubilee of the Year 2000, November 29, 1998.

55. Ibid., p. 179, from Homily at a Mass at Oriole Park at Camden Yards, Baltimore, Maryland, October 8, 1995.

56. John Paul II, *Crossing the Threshold of Hope*, p. 192.

57. "Developing Special Concern for the Homeless," Lent 1997 message for the first year of preparation for the Great Jubilee of the Year 2000.

58. *An Invitation to Joy: Selections from the Writings and Speeches of His Holiness John Paul II*. New York: Simon and Schuster, 1999, p. 42.

Notes

59. *Pope John Paul II, Celebrate the Third Millennium*, p. 169, from *Familiaris Consortio*.
60. Pope John Paul II, *A Pilgrim Pope*, p. 187.
61. Ibid., p. 238.
62. Ibid., p. 250.
63. Ibid., p. 318.
64. "Only Christ Can Fulfill Man's Hopes," November 8, 1995.
65. "God's Fatherhood Is Basis of the Family," The Holy Father's address to those taking part in the 14th plenary assembly of the Pontifical Council for the Family, June 4, 1999.
66. BrainyQuote.com
67. "God's Fatherhood Is Basis of the Family."
68. "Evangelization of Urban Culture Is a Formidable Challenge for the Church."
69. Pope John Paul II, *Forgiveness*, p. 22.
70. Pope John Paul II, *Celebrate the Third Millennium*, p. 71, from Address on the World Day of Peace, December 8, 1996.
71. Frossard and Pope John Paul II, p. 80.
72. BrainyQuote.com.
73. Pope John Paul II, *A Pilgrim Pope*, p. 271.
74. *USA Today*, August 19, 2002.
75. BrainyQuote.com.
76. Weigel, p. 778.
77. *Policy Review*, October/November 2000.
78. "Ad Limina Apostolorum."
79. "Fides et Ratio."
80. Sullivan and the editors of *Life*, p. 44.
81. Ibid., p. 87.
82. January 31, 2001.
83. Apostolic exhortation on reconciliation and penance origin and meaning of the document.
84. Letter to Priests for Holy Thursday 1998.
85. Kwitny, p. 302.
86. Hebblethwaite and Kaufmann, p 44.
87. "Fides et Ratio."
88. Bunson, p. 18.
89. *An Invitation to Joy*, p. 100.
90. John Paul II, *Crossing the Threshold of Hope*, p. 222.
91. Pope John Paul II, *Fear Not*, p. 114.
92. Pope John Paul II, *A Pilgrim Pope*, p. 4.
93. *An Invitation to Joy*, p. 33.
94. "Fides et Ratio."
95. Bunson, p. 120.
96. Pope John Paul II, *Forgiveness*, p. 85.
97. Message to Cardinal William W. Baum, April 1, 2000.
98. *An Invitation to Joy*, p. 53.
99. Pope John Paul II, *Celebrate the Third Millennium*, p. 239, from Message for the Eleventh World Youth Day in 1996, November 26, 1995.
100. *John Paul II: Chronicle of a Remarkable Life*, p. 111.
101. Weigel, p. 810.
102. "Seek to Be Active in Life of Your Local Church, November 9, 1996.
103. "Learn to Love Mary, Our Heavenly Mother," the Holy Father's Address when he visited the Pontifical Roman Major Seminary for its patronal feast day of Our Lady of Trust, March 4, 2000.

104. Apostolic exhortation on reconciliation and penance origin and meaning of the document.

105. Letter to Priests for Holy Thursday 1998.

106. Ibid.

107. Ibid.

108. Kwitny, p. 570.

109. "True Marriage Requires A Reciprocal Gift of Exclusive, Indissoluble, and Fruitful Love Commitment," January 21, 1999.

110. "God's Fatherhood Is Basis of the Family."

111. Weigel, p. 776.

112. "The Freedom of Conscience and of Religion, September 1, 1980.

113. *An Invitation to Joy*, p. 159.

114. Bernstein and Politi, p. 128.

115. Pope John Paul II, *Celebrate the Third Millennium*, p. 28, from Message for the Eleventh World Youth Day in 1996, November 26, 1995.

116. *An Invitation to Joy*, p. 136.

117. "Science Serves Humanity Only When It Is Joined to Conscience," January 11, 1997.

118. Bunson, p. 40.

119. Wojtyla, Karol (John Paul II), *Love and Responsibility* (Originally published in Polish as *Milosc I Odpowiedzialnosc* in 1960). Translated by H. T. Willetts. New York: Farrar, Straus, and Giroux, 1981, p. 46.

120. Pope John Paul II, *A Pilgrim Pope*, p. 227.

121. Apostolic exhortation on reconciliation and penance origin and meaning of the document.

122. John Paul II, *Crossing the Threshold of Hope*, p. 92.

123. Bernstein and Politi, p. 441.

124. Weigel, p. 500.

125. John Paul II, *Crossing the Threshold of Hope*, p. 92–93.

126. Ibid., p. 44.

127. Pope John Paul II, *A Pilgrim Pope*, p. 43.

128. "Communicating Way, Truth, and Life," Holy Father's Message for the 31st World Communications Day (which was celebrated on May 11, 1997).

129. "God Will Judge the World with Justice," November 19, 1996.

130. Homily in the Upper Room, Jerusalem, March 23, 2000.

131. "*Dominicae Cenae*," Letter of the Supreme Pontiff Pope John Paul II to All the Bishops of the Church, February 24, 1980.

132. John Paul II, *Crossing the Threshold of Hope*, p. 45.

133. Pope John Paul II, *Celebrate the Third Millennium*, p. 178, from Address to the youth of Rome in St. Peter's Square, March 20, 1997.

134. Ibid., p. 228, from Message for the Eleventh World Youth Day in 1996, November 26, 1995.

135. Kwitny, p. 325.

136. John Paul II, *Crossing the Threshold of Hope*, p. 6.

137. BrainyQuote.com.

138. Weigel, p. 351.

139. BrainyQuote.com.

140. John Paul II, *Crossing the Threshold of Hope*, p. 99.

141. Weigel, p. 492.

Notes

142. Jubilee of Scientists, May 25, 2000.

143. Wojtyla, p. 55.

144. Sullivan and the editors of Life, p. 119.

145. Pope John Paul II, *Celebrate the Third Millennium*, p. 63, from Address to the Eighth World Youth Day, Denver, Colorado, August 14, 1993.

146. Frossard and Pope John Paul II, p. 100.

147. Jubilee of Scientists, May 25, 2000.

148. Pope John Paul II, *A Pilgrim Pope*, p. 96.

149. To the Pontifical Academy for Life, February 14, 1997.

150. Bunson, p. 57.

151. Pope John Paul II, *A Pilgrim Pope*, p. 30.

152. Bunson, p. 76.

153. Weigel, p. 101.

154. Pope John Paul II, *A Pilgrim Pope*, p. 153.

155. Wojtyla, p. 135.

156. Ibid., p. 183.

157. Ibid., p. 29.

158. Jubilee of Migrants and Itinerant People, June 2, 2000.

159. Wojtyla, p. 34.

160. "On the Dignity and Vocation of Women," September 30, 1988.

161. Pope John Paul II, *A Pilgrim Pope*, p. 67.

162. BrainyQuote.com.

163. Pope John Paul II, *A Pilgrim Pope*, p. 67.

164. Frossard and Pope John Paul II, p. 119.

165. Pope John Paul II, *A Pilgrim Pope*, p. 165.

166. Holy Father's Message for the 31st World Communications Day, May 11, 1997.

167. Pope John Paul II, *Celebrate the Third Millennium*, p. 14, from Message for the Thirty-first World Communications Day, January 24, 1997.

168. Frossard and Pope John Paul II, p. 218.

169. Apostolic exhortation on reconciliation and penance origin and meaning of the document.

170. Pope John Paul II, *Forgiveness*, p. 35.

171. Letter to Priests, Holy Thursday 2001.

172. Pope John Paul II, *Forgiveness*, p. 67.

173. Ad Limina Address to the Bishops of Texas, Oklahoma, and Arkansas, June 6, 1998.

174. Kwitny, p. 361.

175. Wojtyla, p. 253.

176. Pope John Paul II, *A Pilgrim Pope*, p. 214.

177. BrainyQuote.com.

178. Frossard and Pope John Paul II, p. 143.

179. Ad Limina Address to the Bishops of Texas, Oklahoma, and Arkansas.

180. Ibid.

181. *An Invitation to Joy*, p. 51.

182. Address to members of the Roman Curia at the annual exchange of Christmas greetings, December 21, 1996.

183. "Mary Is Model of Christian Life," the Holy Father's Letter to Archbishop of Nguyen Nhu The of Hue, Viet Nam, marking the closure of the Marian Year, July 16, 1999.

184. Weigel, p. 818.
185. "Mother Teresa: A Model of Gospel Service," *Angelus*, September 5, 1999.
186. "Motherhood: Woman's Gift to Society," Holy Father addresses international meeting on promoting the well-being of women, December 7, 1996.
187. Bunson, p. 178.
188. Kwitny, p. 246.
189. Weigel, p. 310.
190. Kwitny, p. 17.
191. Hebblethwaite and Kaufmann, p. 89.
192. Sullivan and the editors of *Life*, p. 83.
193. Hebblethwaite and Kaufmann, p. 89.
194. Weigel, p. 317.
195. Kwitny, p. 552.
196. *John Paul II: Chronicle of a Remarkable Life*, p. 111, 2000.
197. "Let Us Give Children a Future of Peace," World Day of Peace, January 1, 1996.
198. *"Dominicae Cenae."*
199. Apostolic exhortation on reconciliation and penance origin and meaning of the document.
200. Ibid.
201. "God Will Judge the World with Justice," November 19, 1996.
202. "To Congress on Integration of Disabled Children," January 5, 2000.
203. "You have the Words of Eternal Life," Message to Young People for the 11th World Youth Day in 1996.
204. *"Fides et Ratio."*
205. Ibid.
206. Ibid.
207. Ibid.
208. BrainyQuote.com.
209. *USA Today*, August 19, 2002.
210. Ibid.
211. Frossard and Pope John Paul II, p. 152.
212. *An Invitation to Joy*, p. 169.
213. Bunson, p. 130.
214. *An Invitation to Joy*, p. 108.
215. "Malice of Sinner vs. Goodness of Lord," General Audience, August 22, 2001.
216. "Never Tire of Teaching the Ideals of Christian Marriage and Family Life," the Holy Father's Address to the Bishops of Kenya, who were making their ad limina visit to Rome, May 20, 1999.
217. Bunson, p. 125.
218. Pope John Paul II, *Celebrate the Third Millennium*, p. 37, from Ad limina address to the bishops of New England, September 21, 1993.
219. Kwitny, p. 70.
220. Weigel, p. 224.
221. Pope John Paul II, *Celebrate the Third Millennium*, p. 41, from *Dominum et Vivicantem*, May 18, 1986.
222. Ibid.
223. *"Ad limina Apostolorum"*: Bishops' Conference of France I, January 11, 1997.
224. BrainyQuote.com.
225. "God's Grace Will Nourish Your Love," address to members of the Roman Curia at the annual exchange of Christmas greetings, December 21, 1996.

226. BrainyQuote.com.

227. "Never Tire of Teaching the Ideals of Christian Marriage and Family Life," the Holy Father's address to the Bishops of Kenya who were making their ad limina visit to Rome, May 20, 1999.

228. "*Ad limina Apostolorum*": Bishops' Conference of France 2, pastoral and theological activity of priests must begin with prayer.

229. Bernstein and Politi, p. 508.

230. "*Ad limina Apostolorum*": Bishops' Conference of France 2, pastoral and theological activity of priests must begin with prayer.

231. Ibid.

232. Apostolic exhortation on reconciliation and penance origin and meaning of the document.

233. Ibid.

234. Bunson, p. 67.

235. John Paul II, *Crossing the Threshold of Hope*, p. 206.

236. Moody, p. 160.

237. "Fetus as a Patient," Discourse to International Congress, April 3, 2000.

238. "On Combatting Abortion and Euthanasia," Letter of Pope John Paul II to all the world's bishops, May 19, 1991.

239. *Policy Review*, October/November 2000.

240. Weigel, p. 801.

241. "*Dies Domini*," Apostolic letter of the holy father John Paul II to the bishops, clergy, and faithful of the Catholic Church on keeping the Lord's Day holy.

242. Ibid.

243. Ibid.

244. Pope John Paul II, *Celebrate the Third Millennium*, p. 166, from Dies Domini, Pentecost Sunday, May 31, 1998.

245. "We Must Follow Jesus," Homily for Second Sunday of Lent, February 23, 1997.

246. Ibid.

247. John Paul II, *Crossing the Threshold of Hope*, p. 73.

248. Ibid., p. 21.

249. Ibid., p. 139.

250. Pope John Paul II, *Fear Not*, p. 90.

251. Bernstein and Politi, p. 380.

252. Evangelization of Urban Culture Is a Formidable Challenge for the Church

253. Kwitny, p. 327.

254. "*Fides et Ratio*."

255. Kwitny, p. 342.

256. "Mentally Ill Are Also Made in God's Image," November 30, 1997.

257. Sullivan and the editors of *Life*, p. 87.

258. Frossard and Pope John Paul II, p. 83.

259. "Mentally Ill Are Also Made in God's Image."

260. "On the Dignity and Vocation of Women."

261. Pope John Paul II, *Fear Not*, p. 28.

262. "Baptism Saves Us from Slavery to Sin," January 12, 1997.

263. "I Was in Prison and You Came to Me," Homily on visit to Regina Coeli Prison, July 9, 2000.

264. Apostolic exhortation on reconciliation and penance origin and meaning of the document.

265. Ibid.

266. Ibid.

267. Letter to Priests, Holy Thursday 2001.

268. "I Was in Prison and You Came to Me."

269. Ibid.

270. *John Paul II: Chronicle of a Remarkable Life*, p. 124, 2000.

271. Kwitny, p. 567.

272. "Mother Teresa: A Model of Gospel Service."

273. Pope John Paul II, *A Pilgrim Pope*, p. 124.

274. *An Invitation to Joy*, p. 172.

275. Pope John Paul II, *A Pilgrim Pope*, p. 203.

276. *Ad Limina* Address to the Bishops of Texas, Oklahoma, and Arkansas.

277. Homily at Jubilee of Sports People, October 29, 2000.

278. Ibid.

279. *John Paul II: Chronicle of a Remarkable Life*, p. 93.

280. Kwitny, p. 198.

281. Homily at Jubilee of Sports People.

282. Bunson, p. 7.

283. John Paul II, *Crossing the Threshold of Hope*, p. 25.

284. Pope John Paul II, *A Pilgrim Pope*, p. 306.

285. Wojtyla, p. 87.

286. "*Fides et Ratio*."

287. Pope John Paul II, *Celebrate the Third Millennium*, p. 103, from Address to the youth of Rome in St. Peter's Square, March 20, 1997.

288. "*Fides et Ratio*."

289. *Ad Limina* Address to the Bishops of Texas, Oklahoma, and Arkansas.

290. Frossard and Pope John Paul II, p. 165.

291. Kwitny, p. 214.

292. Moody, p. 102.

293. BrainyQuote.com.

294. *An Invitation to Joy*, p. 188.

295. Frossard and Pope John Paul II, p. 32.

296. Kwitny, p. 620.

297. Ibid., p. 136.

298. "On the Dignity and Vocation of Women."

299. Weigel, p. 580.

300. Weigel, p. 767.

301. *An Invitation to Joy*, p. 60.

302. "On the Dignity and Vocation of Women."

303. John Paul II, *Crossing the Threshold of Hope*, p. 217.

304. Bunson, p. 173.

305. Ibid., p. 179.

306. "Lord, Give Success to Work of Our Hands," Homily for Jubilee of Workers, May 1, 2000.

307. Ibid.

308. Hebblethwaite and Kaufmann, p. 105.

309. BrainyQuote.com.

310. Bunson, p. 7.

311. *John Paul II: Chronicle of a Remarkable Life*, p. 38.

312. Weigel, p. 419.

313. *Policy Review*, October/November 2000, from *Sollicitudo Rei Socialis (On Social Concerns)*.

314. BrainyQuote.com.

315. *An Invitation to Joy*, p. 126.

316. Weigel, p. 683.

317. *Newsweek*, April 10, 1995.

318. "On Human Work," Encyclical Letter on the Ninetieth Anniversary of Rerum Novarum.

319. Pope John Paul II, *Celebrate the Third Millennium*, p. 20, from Letter to the Bishops of the United States, June 11, 1993.

320. Kwitny, p. 388.

321. "*Fides et Ratio.*"

322. Wojtyla, p. 229.

323. BrainyQuote.com.

324. "The Freedom of Conscience and Religion," September 1, 1980.

325. "Sunday Mass Is a Serious Obligation," Angelus, August 9, 1998.

326. "*Dominicae Cenae,*" Letter to all the Bishops of the Church, February 24, 1980.

327. "The Freedom of Conscience and Religion," September 1, 1980.

328. "Let Us Give Children a Future of Peace."

329. Moody, p. 48.

330. *An Invitation to Joy*, p. 37.

331. John Paul II, *Crossing the Threshold of Hope*, p. 124.

332. BrainyQuote.com.

333. Bernstein and Politi, p. 19.

334. *John Paul II: Chronicle of a Remarkable Life*, p. 21.

335. Kwitny, p. 214.

336. Ibid., p. 37.

337. *Biography*, September 2000.

338. Sullivan and the editors of *Life*, p. 24.

339. Moody, p. 15.

340. Ibid.p. 28.

341. Hebblethwaite and Kaufmann, p. 38.

342. Kwitny, p. 67.

343. Weigel, p. 105.

344. Kwitny, p. xii.

345. Moody, p. 59.

346. Ibid., p. 34.

347. *Christian Science Monitor*, October 12, 2000.

348. *John Paul II: Chronicle of a Remarkable Life*, p. 78.

349. Frossard and Pope John Paul II, p. 62.

350. *John Paul II: Chronicle of a Remarkable Life*, p. 63.

351. Moody, p. 66.

352. Hebblethwaite and Kaufmann, p. 78.

353. Kwitny, p. 6.

354. *Christian Science Monitor*, October 12, 2000.

355. Weigel, p. 298.

356. Ibid., p. 301.

357. World and I, December 1997, from *Crossing the Threshold of Hope*.

358. *New Perspectives Quarterly*, Fall 1998.

359. Ibid.

360. *Canadian Dimension*, May/June 1998.

361. Bernstein and Politi, p. 294.

362. Frossard and Pope John Paul II, p. 229.

363. Kwitny, p. 208.

364. Ibid., p. 333.

365. Hebblethwaite, and Kaufmann, p. 120.

366. Moody, p. 147.

367. BrainyQuote.com.

368. Sullivan and the editors of *Life*, p. 63.

369. Weigel, p. 211.

370. *U.S. News and World Report*, May 11, 1998.